WHOLLY**KIDS**

ISBN 978-1-4158-7319-9
Item 5490111

Dewey Decimal Classification Number: 259.22
Subject Heading: CHURCH WORK WITH CHILDREN\CHRISTIAN
EDUCATION\RELIGIOUS EDUCATION

Printed in the United States of America

Kids Ministry Publishing
LifeWay Church Resources
One LifeWay Plaza
Nashville, Tennessee 37234-0172

We believe the Bible has God for its author; salvation for its end; and truth,
without any mixture of error, for its matter and that all Scripture is totally
true and trustworthy. To review LifeWay's doctrinal guideline, please visit
www.lifeway.com/doctrinalguideline.

All Scripture quotations are taken from the Holman Christian Standard
Bible®, copyright 1999, 2000, 2002, 2003, 2009 by Holman Bible
Publishers. Used by permission.

Special Thanks:
Katy Bradley, Stephanie Salvatore, Alyssa Jones, Jessica Shippen

From the Editor ...

TUCK

Despite the numerous reasons I could give you why this book is important to you and to kids ministry, I'd like to show you my four most important reasons. **REED** is my serious athlete son who knows how to have a good time. **NASH** is my do-anything-for-a-laugh, nurturing son whose dimples will melt the hardest of hearts. **WILL** is my mover and shaker son who never ceases showering people with his trademark, slobbery-blown kisses. **TUCK** is my easy-going, quickly-growing baby boy who is following his brothers' footsteps of growing up much faster than I am prepared for. So, what are your reasons' names? Is she the freckled faced girl in your Sunday School class or the rambunctious boy in your minivan? We all have reasons why this book is important. As you read this book, I hope the descriptions and images will bring to mind all of the names of the kids in your life who need you in theirs.

Jeff Land,
Contributing Editor

REED

WILL

NASH

LifeWay Kids Ministry Specialists

BY THE NUMBERS: Kids ministry specialists **JERRY VOGEL**, **BILL EMEOTT**, and **KLISTA STORTS** weigh in on why ministry to kids is important and how it has impacted their own lives.

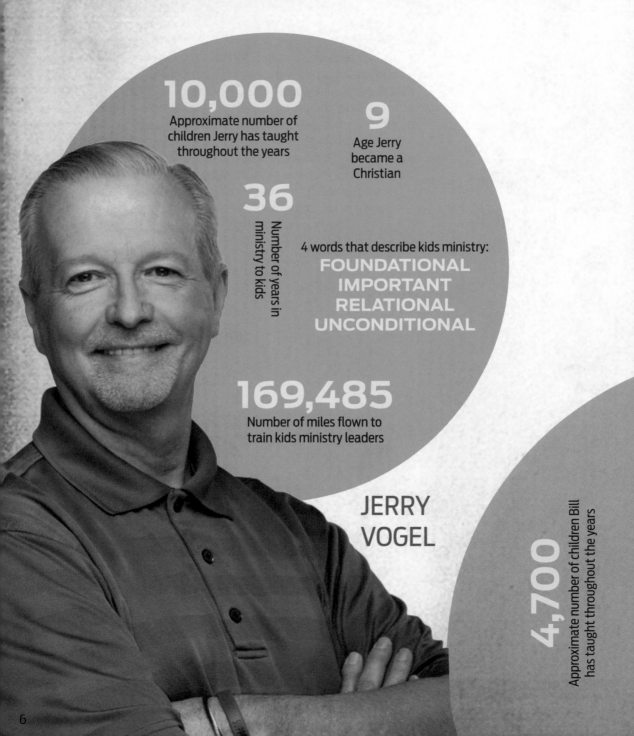

10,000
Approximate number of children Jerry has taught throughout the years

9
Age Jerry became a Christian

36
Number of years in ministry to kids

4 words that describe kids ministry:
FOUNDATIONAL
IMPORTANT
RELATIONAL
UNCONDITIONAL

169,485
Number of miles flown to train kids ministry leaders

JERRY VOGEL

4,700
Approximate number of children Bill has taught throughout the years

KLISTA STORTS

22

Number of years in ministry to kids

Why this book is important:
"IT'S A GREAT REMINDER THAT GOD CREATED EACH CHILD UNIQUELY AND WE NEED TO TEACH WITH THAT IN MIND."

50

Approximate number of candy-filled mugs Klista's received as Christmas gifts

1,243

Approximate number of children Klista has taught throughout the years

Single greatest piece of advice received as a kid's ministry leader:
"IF A CHILD LEAVES KNOWING JESUS LOVES HIM BECAUSE YOU'VE LOVED HIM, YOU'RE DOING SOMETHING RIGHT."

23

Number of years in ministry to kids

328,464

Number of miles flown to train kids ministry leaders

BILL EMEOTT

Single greatest piece of advice received as a kid's ministry leader:

"KIDS LEARN BEST FROM THE OVER-FLOW OF WHAT GOD HAS TAUGHT YOU."

10

Age when Bill became a Christian

TABLE OF
CONTENTS

PRESCHOOL
CHARACTERISTICS

Preschoolers learn, grow, and develop at different paces. The following information can be considered benchmarks for what a preschooler may be capable of at this age.

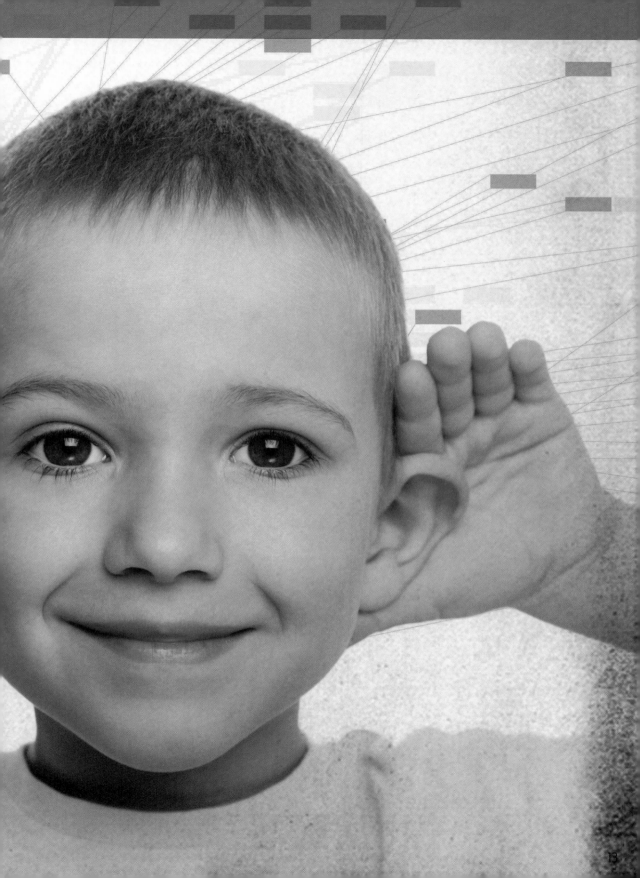

PHYSICAL

- use many complex reflexes
- begin to reach toward objects
- hold up their heads
- sit without support
- roll over, crawl
- look for dropped toys

Babies

MENTAL

- use senses to learn
- cry to signal pain or distress
- recognize principle caregivers
- use vocal and non-vocal communication
- react differently to familiar and unfamiliar
- know and respond to name

SOCIAL/EMOTIONAL

- smile broadly at others
- show alertness when spoken to
- begin to initiate social interchange
- become quiet in unfamiliar settings
- make eye contact
- show interest in other children

SPIRITUAL

- develop a sense of trust as needs are met consistently
- sense attitudes and expressions of love
- learn to associate God's name with love and trust
- sense importance associated with Jesus and the Bible
- point to the Bible and pictures of Jesus

PHYSICAL

- sit well in chairs
- climb
- love to explore
- draw on paper with markers
- carry objects from place to place
- move constantly

Ones

MENTAL

- remember simple events
- begin to group familiar objects
- use trial and error in learning
- can label body parts
- understand and use words for items
- try to make themselves understood

SOCIAL/EMOTIONAL

- experience stranger anxiety
- play simple games
- can practice taking turns
- like to exert control
- recognize emotions of others
- imitate household actions

SPIRITUAL

- begin to make simple choices
- continue to grow in trust of adults
- begin to distinguish between acceptable and unacceptable behavior
- begin to recognize pictures of Jesus

MENTAL

- use 5 to 300 words
- begin using sentences
- identify themselves by gender
- follow simple directions in order
- match, compare, group, and sort items
- enjoy repetition
- begin using numbers
- repeat songs
- know colors

SOCIAL/EMOTIONAL

- take interest in family
- try to help
- initiate play with peers
- show love and affection
- respond to the moods of others
- use imagination
- strongly assert independence

SPIRITUAL

- sing simple songs about God and Jesus
- say thank You to God
- listen to Bible stories

PHYSICAL

- develop preference for right or left hand
- stand on one foot and balance
- jump on tiptoes
- walk between parallel lines
- have better gross motor coordination
- have difficulty relaxing
- help undress themselves

MENTAL

- use 300 to 1,000 words
- learn short songs
- display creativity and imagination
- experience fears and bad dreams
- begin speaking in complete sentences
- do one thing at a time
- want to know what things are and how they work

SOCIAL/EMOTIONAL

- try to please adults; conform more often
- begin to show some self-control, but resort to temper tantrums when extremely angry
- take turns more readily
- like to hear themselves talk
- respond to verbal guidance and enjoy encouragement
- play cooperatively with others
- have imaginary companions

SPIRITUAL

- identify some Bible characters and stories
- recognize the Bible as a special book; enjoy handling and using the Bible
- enjoy singing songs about the Bible, family, nature, friends at church
- understand that God, Jesus, and church are special
- begin to develop a conscience and are sensitive to feelings of shame and guilt

PHYSICAL

- use large muscles
- dress themselves fairly easily
- display some fine motor skills
- notice the differences in boys and girls
- dislike nap time and have difficulty sleeping during this time

MENTAL

- use 500 to 2,000 words
- can remember name and address
- have increased attention span
- can do two things at once
- are highly imaginative;
  cannot separate fact and fantasy
- show a curiosity about life cycle
- understand time concepts better
- enjoy being silly
- use many words without knowing their meanings

PHYSICAL

- show good large muscle coordination
- develop a longer, leaner body
- develop fine motor control for painting,
  drawing, and cutting with scissors
- walk backward
- need a high level of physical activity
- exhibit right- and left-handedness
- enjoy building materials with parts to
  assemble

SPIRITUAL

- like to retell Bible stories
- enjoy Bible verse games
- recognize that God and Jesus love people and
  help people in special ways
- accept responsibility for helping people
- exhibit a conscience
- express love for God and Jesus
- may show concern for others
- can sing songs about Jesus

Fours

SOCIAL/EMOTIONAL

- have total confidence in their own abilities
- bossy; show great independence
- tattle frequently
- focus on cooperative play and take turns
- like to be helpers if they initiate the idea
- respond to reason, humor, and firmness
- play cooperatively with other children

23

YOUNGER KIDS

CHARACTERISTICS

Younger kids are learning how they fit into the world. They begin to take on responsibilities. Remember that although characteristics for a particular age group may be considered typical, every child grows and develops at different rates.

MENTAL

- print their name but not too clearly
- name most uppercase letters
- utilize a 2,000-word vocabulary
- say numbers *1* to *20*
- know morning from afternoon
- are challenged by new tasks
- seek explanations concerning why and how
- begin to recognize basic reading words
- enjoy classification, sequencing, and sorting

SOCIAL/EMOTIONAL

- get along well in small groups
- comfort friends who are upset
- have best friends, but change friends often
- may be prone to self-criticism and guilt
- may continue to express fears
- enjoy imitating adults
- begin to distinguish truth from lies
- enjoy competition
- can accept responsibility

PHYSICAL

- skip well; hop in a straight line
- cut well with scissors
- exhibit well-established right- or left-handedness
- begin cutting permanent teeth
- have good hand-eye coordination
- dress themselves
- can control their large muscles
- develop appetites for favorite foods

Fives

B
1
2
3
4
5
6
7
8
9
10
11
12

SPIRITUAL

- remember and like to tell Bible stories
- use the Bible and like to find Bible phrases/verses
- like to take care of God's world
- begin to ask questions about God
- can make life application of Bible verses
- continue to develop a conscience

SPIRITUAL

- see Jesus as a friend and helper
- may enjoy praying
- like learning from the Bible
- may know many basic Bible stories
- may make conclusions about God
- may begin to understand truth and honesty, right from wrong; may not make personal application
- may begin to recognize fantasy as fantasy
- may begin to have a simple understanding of sin
- may begin to have a simple understanding of the gospel
- may be easily manipulated by a desire to please adults
- know the right answers, but may not understand application

Sixes

MENTAL

- may like to work
- may like to explain things; show-and-tell is useful
- may love jokes and guessing games
- love to ask questions
- like new games, ideas
- love to color, paint
- learn best through discovery
- enjoy process more than product
- try more than they can accomplish (eyes bigger than stomach)
- recognize representative symbols as more important
- begin to understand past when tied closely to present
- interested in skill and technique for its own sake

SOCIAL/EMOTIONAL

- want to be first
- are competitive; enthusiastic
- are sometimes a poor sport or dishonest; invent rules
- are anxious to do well
- view any failure as hard; thrive on encouragement
- can be bossy, teasing, critical of others
- are easily upset when hurt
- view friends as important (may have a best friend)
- complain frequently

PHYSICAL

- are sloppy, in a hurry; speed is a benchmark
- are noisy in classroom
- are learning to distinguish left from right
- may struggle with fine motor skills
- tire easily
- suffer frequent illness
- enjoy outdoors, gym

SPIRITUAL

- may begin to put Bible stories into sequence
- may begin to understand the relationship between the Old and New Testaments
- may be interested in finding out more about God and Jesus
- may understand that Jesus is God's Son and begin to understand what that means
- may ask why God would let Jesus die for the wrong things that everyone else does
- may recognize consequences for their sin
- may begin to realize that God forgives when asked
- may understand that people become Christians by accepting Jesus as Savior and Lord

PHYSICAL

- work may be more tidy, neat
- sometimes tense
- like confined space
- experience many hurts, real and imagined
- improve fine motor skills
- use pincer grasp and pencil point

Sevens

MENTAL

- like to work
- are interested in all sorts of codes
- like to review learning
- need closure, must complete assignments
- may like to work slowly and alone
- may like to be read to
- may have growing reflective ability
- erase constantly, want work to be perfect
- like to repeat tasks
- like board games
- want to discover how things work; like to take things apart

SOCIAL/EMOTIONAL

- don't like to make mistakes or to risk making them
- are sometimes moody, depressed, sulking, or shy
- need security and structure
- rely on teacher for help
- are sensitive to others' feelings
- are conscientious and serious
- need constant reinforcement
- have strong likes and dislikes
- are good listeners and precise talkers
- like to send notes

Eights

MENTAL

- like to experiment and find out how things are made
- vary with peers in reading ability
- value money
- are eager to learn

SOCIAL/EMOTIONAL

- like peers of the same sex and dislike the opposite sex
- are eager to please and want to be liked by peers and adults
- boys shout; girls giggle and whisper
- idolize heroes
- like to work with others

SPIRITUAL

- ask serious questions about religion
- are developing values
- can be truthful and honest
- often have difficulty making decisions

PHYSICAL

- have good hand-eye coordination
- may overdo it with physical activities and have trouble calming down

OLDER KIDS
CHARACTERISTICS

Older kids are rapidly reaching puberty and have well-developed vocabulary and thinking skills. In terms of spiritual characteristics, it is important to remember some older kids have not had the benefit of foundational spiritual education.

SPIRITUAL

- are often beginning to feel the need for a Savior
- are growing conscious of themselves and of sin
- want to do things the right way and may feel ashamed when wrong
- think in terms of right and wrong more than good and evil

Nines

MENTAL

- have lengthening attention span
- are able to be involved in experiences that deal with feelings and thinking
- accept carefully worded criticism
- are beginning to think abstractly

SOCIAL/EMOTIONAL

- need to be able to let off steam and may take out feelings on others
- are interested in own community and country
- are beginning to feel that the group is as important as self
- are great talkers and need to be allowed to talk
- change moods quickly

PHYSICAL

- like to draw and sketch
- have slow, steady growth and good muscle control
- girls' bodies usually develop more quickly than boys

SPIRITUAL

- are developing concepts of love and trust
- are developing a conscience and a value system

Tens

MENTAL

- are continuing to think abstractly
- are imaginative, creative, and curious
- have developed basic reading and writing skills
- can express ideas, understand cause and effect, solve problems, and plan

SOCIAL/EMOTIONAL

- are motivated most by own interest and think of themselves, using own experiences
- can operate comfortably within a group
- like acceptance and encouragement; can become easily discouraged

PHYSICAL

- like to use abundant energy and physical skills

MENTAL

- are capable of deep thoughts
- can cope with success and failure
- can concentrate when interested
- think quickly and memorize easily

SPIRITUAL

- have formed concepts of personal worth
- are ready for spiritual answers and directions
- can make many choices, but may not follow through on long-term commitments

PHYSICAL

- have good coordination and muscle skills

Elevens

SOCIAL/ EMOTIONAL

- can accept rules, organization, responsibilities, and leader-follower roles
- like to win and improve on achievements
- recognize and appreciate individual differences

41

SPIRITUAL

- feel deeply about own experiences; can be sensitive to others
- beginning to adopt a religious belief system of their own

Twelves

MENTAL

- can distinguish between fact and fiction
- can accept and work toward short-term goals
- can discern time and space relationships

SOCIAL/EMOTIONAL

- are aware of sex roles; have changing attitudes toward the opposite sex
- have deep need for companionship and approval of peers
- are ready for responsibilities and opportunities for self-direction
- are easily influenced emotionally and can cope with some feelings

PHYSICAL

- are approaching puberty; girls usually ahead of boys

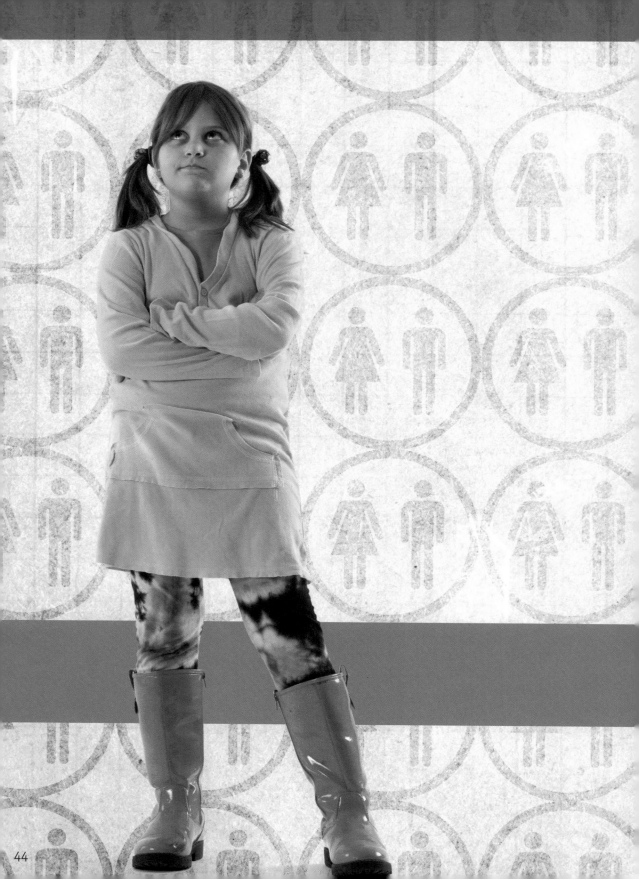

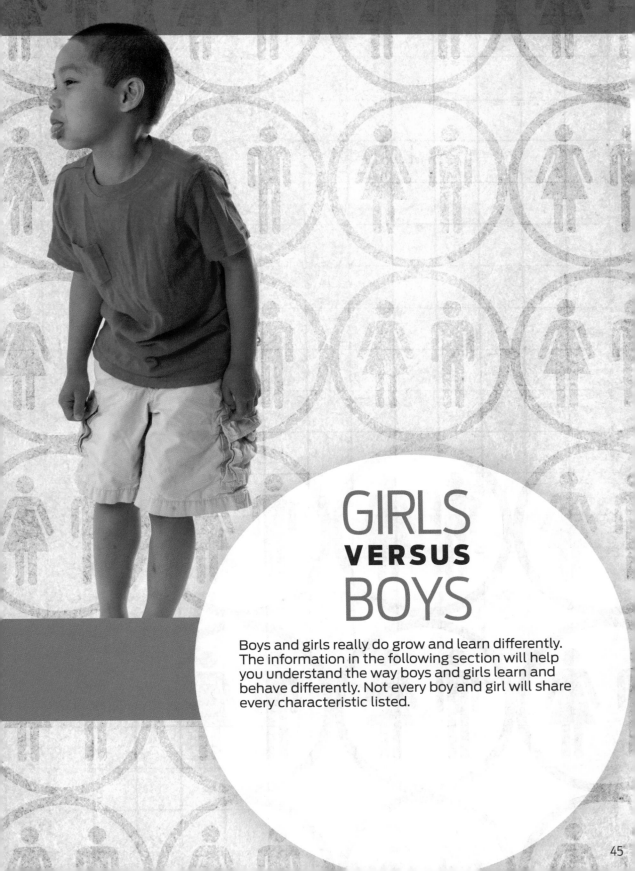

GIRLS **VERSUS** BOYS

Boys and girls really do grow and learn differently. The information in the following section will help you understand the way boys and girls learn and behave differently. Not every boy and girl will share every characteristic listed.

FOCUS

GIRLS ARE MORE ABLE TO FOCUS WHEN THEY ARE SITTING IN A WARMER ROOM.

RISK

GIRLS MAY SHY AWAY FROM RISK.

VISUAL APPEAL

GIRLS ARE DRAWN MORE TOWARD COLORS.

Focus, Risk, & Visual Appeal

FOCUS

BOYS ARE MORE ABLE TO FOCUS WHEN THEY ARE STANDING IN A COOLER ROOM.

RISK

BOYS TEND TO BE MORE DARING.

VISUAL APPEAL

BOYS ARE DRAWN TOWARD MOVING OBJECTS.

DOG

LEARNING

**GIRLS OFTEN
LEARN BETTER
THROUGH WORDS.**

READING

**GIRLS ENJOY
READING
AND WRITING.**

MOTOR SKILLS

**GIRLS DEVELOP
FINE MOTOR SKILLS
EARLY.**

Learning, Reading, & Motor Skills

LEARNING

**BOYS OFTEN
LEARN BETTER
THROUGH PICTURES.**

READING

**BOYS AVOID
READING
AND WRITING.**

MOTOR SKILLS

**BOYS DEVELOP
FINE MOTOR SKILLS
LATER.**

GROUPS

GIRLS CAN THRIVE IN LARGER GROUPS.

BOOKS

GIRLS FIND FICTION BOOKS INTERESTING.

FOCUS

GIRLS CAN STAY FOCUSED FOR LONG PERIODS EACH DAY.

Groups, Books, & Focus

GROUPS

**BOYS LEARN
BEST IN
SMALLER GROUPS.**

BOOKS

**BOYS PREFER BOOKS
THAT ARE ABOUT
REAL THINGS OR EVENTS.**

FOCUS

**BOYS WILL ZONE
OUT SEVERAL
TIMES EACH DAY.**

SPATIAL MEMORY

**GIRLS HAVE LESS DEVELOPED
SPATIAL MEMORY.**

GROWTH

**GIRLS GROW
MORE STEADILY
AND CONSISTENTLY.**

FEELINGS

**GIRLS SHOW EMOTION
AND CARE ABOUT
PEOPLE'S FEELINGS.**

Spatial Memory, Growth, & Feelings

SPATIAL MEMORY

BOYS CAN MORE EASILY REMEMBER WHERE THINGS ARE PLACED.

GROWTH

BOYS GROW IN SPURTS AND ARE BEHIND GIRLS THROUGHOUT MOST OF CHILDHOOD.

FEELINGS

BOYS CARE LESS ABOUT FEELINGS AND PEOPLE.

SOCIOECONOMIC
FACTORS

It is important to remember that kids come from all walks of life. Kids can be affected by their income background. This section should help you remember to consider how children from families of different income levels react to different situations or scenarios.

LOWER

MAY NEED TO
BE MOTIVATED

AVERAGE INCOME

USUALLY HAVE
SUPPORTIVE
PARENTAL
INVOLVEMENT

HIGHER

CAN TAKE
OPPORTUNITIES
FOR GRANTED

WHAT
KIDS
THINK
ABOUT
EDUCATION

Education: Be careful not to imply that all kids are from the same educational background. Don't make judgments about different types of schooling.

Rules: Carefully explain rules and assert that rules are for the good of everyone.

Heroes: Remember that some kids want to be just like you and some want to be famous. Don't push a kid to have an unrealistic hero or deflate them by demeaning their goals.

MINISTRY IMPLICATIONS

HIGHER

AVERAGE INCOME

LOWER

HIGHER

AVERAGE INCOME

LOWER

MAY SEEM TO DISREGARD RULES

KNOW WHY RULES EXIST

CAN SEE RULES AS A MEANS OF HINDRANCE

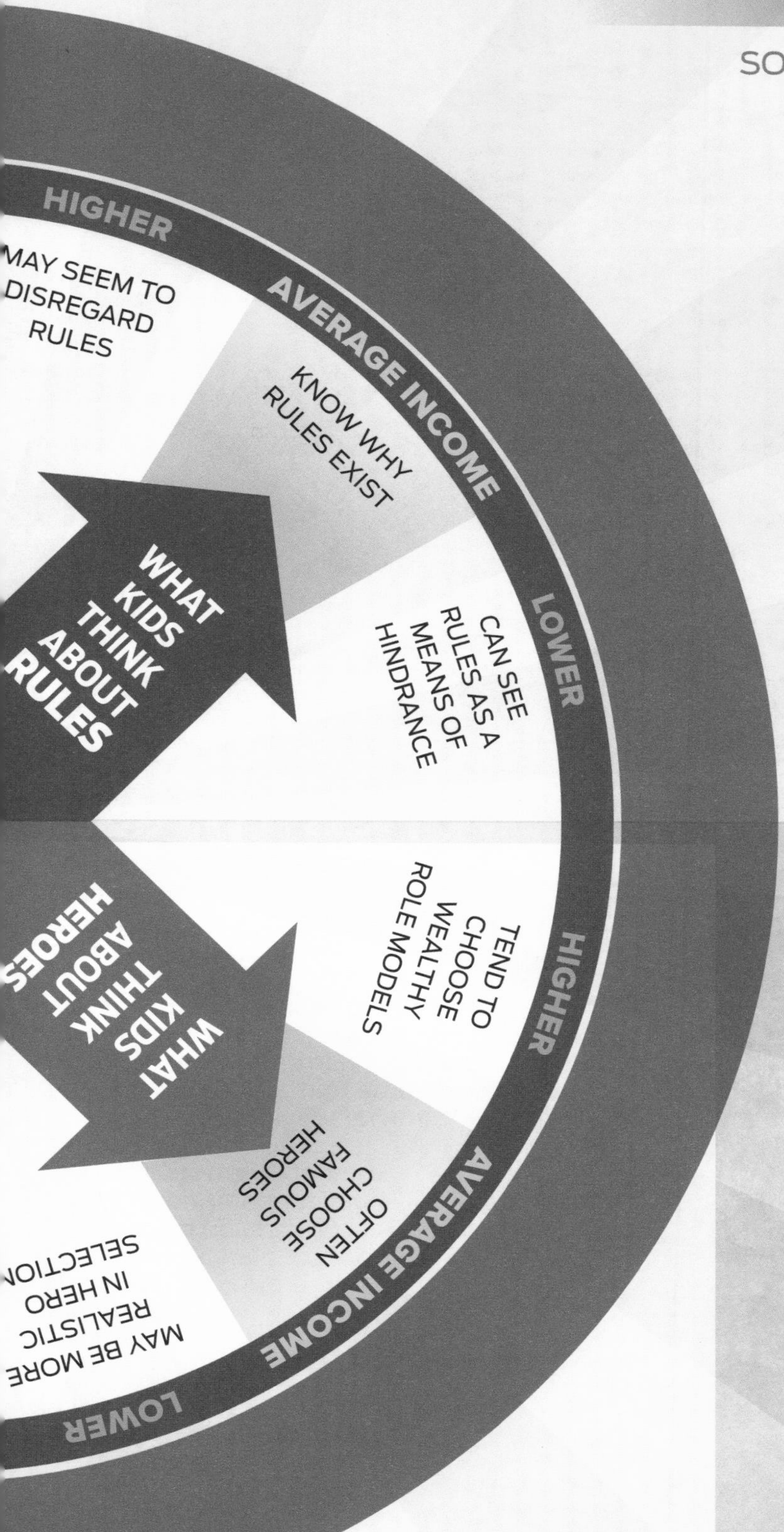

WHAT KIDS THINK ABOUT RULES

TEND TO CHOOSE WEALTHY ROLE MODELS

OFTEN CHOOSE FAMOUS HEROES

WHAT KIDS THINK ABOUT HEROES

MAY BE MORE REALISTIC IN HERO SELECTION

WHAT KIDS THINK ABOUT CLOTHES

LOWER

MAY HAVE 1 OR 2 NICE THINGS HE WEARS OFT*

AVERAGE INCOME

MAY COMPARE HIS CLOTHES TO THOSE WHO HAVE MORE

HIGHER

ALMOST ALWAYS COMES TO CHURCH IN SOMETHING NEW

MINISTRY IMPLICATIONS

Clothes: Don't make comments like "You always have on something new" or "You wore that last week."

Christmas: Remember that all parents have different opinions about Christmas giving. Don't assume that all kids will be showered with gifts.

Special Events: Offer a way for parents or kids to contact you privately for scholarships. Never offer a cost-event without offering scholarships.

Stuff

WHAT KIDS THINK ABOUT CHRISTMAS

HIGHER
MAY BRAG ABOUT RECEIVING LOTS OF LOOT

AVERAGE INCOME
MAY OR MAY NOT RECEIVE MANY GIFTS

LOWER
CAN BE SENSITIVE TO THE AMOUNT OF TOYS RECEIVED BY PEERS

WHAT KIDS THINK ABOUT SPECIAL EVENTS

HIGHER
MAY PLACE HIGHER VALUE ON EVENTS THAT COST SOMETHING

AVERAGE INCOME
STRUGGLE TO KEEP UP WITH TOO MANY OPTIONS

LOWER
MAY NOT HAVE FUNDS FOR EVENTS THAT COST

AVERAGE INCOME

LOWER

MAY HAVE MANY PEOPLE LIVING IN THE SAME HOME

HAS DEFINITE OPINIONS OF STEPSIBLINGS

HIGHER

MAY PLAY PARENTS AGAINST EACH OTHER

WHAT KIDS THINK ABOUT MY **BLENDED FAMILY**

Blended Family: Remember that some kids will attend biweekly because they are visiting the other parent.

Single Parent: Be sensitive to parental holidays like Mother's Day and Father's Day. Don't assume every child has someone for whom they can make a card.

Traditional Family: Avoid verbiage that implies traditional families are preferred over other family types.

MINISTRY IMPLICATIONS

HIGHER

MAY NOT UNDERSTAND PARENTS REASON FOR DIVORCE

AVERAGE INCOME

MAY KNOW REASON FOR PARENT'S DIVORCE

LOWER

MAY HAVE NEVER MET FATHER

WHAT KIDS THINK ABOUT MY DIVORCED OR SINGLE PARENT FAMILY

WHAT KIDS THINK ABOUT MY TRADITIONAL FAMILY

HIGHER

MAY SEEM LIKE FAMILY HAS ITS ALL TOGETHER

AVERAGE INCOME

MAY HAVE SEVERAL SIBLINGS

LOWER

MAY LIVE WITH EXTENDED FAMILY MEMBERS

61

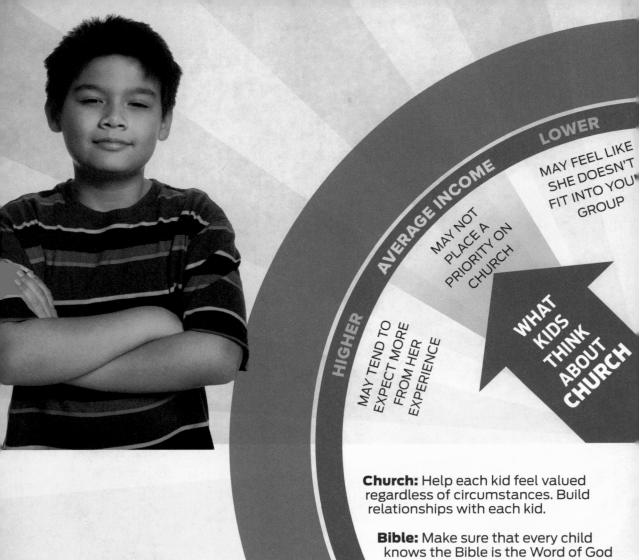

LOWER

MAY FEEL LIKE SHE DOESN'T FIT INTO YOUR GROUP

AVERAGE INCOME

MAY NOT PLACE A PRIORITY ON CHURCH

HIGHER

MAY TEND TO EXPECT MORE FROM HER EXPERIENCE

WHAT KIDS THINK ABOUT CHURCH

Church: Help each kid feel valued regardless of circumstances. Build relationships with each kid.

Bible: Make sure that every child knows the Bible is the Word of God and has access. Help build Bible skils.

God: Share personal experiences in which God has been real and evident. Avoid presenting God as "Mr. Fix-it."

MINISTRY IMPLICATIONS

HIGHER

MAY BRING BIBLE TO CLASS ON ELECTRONIC DEVICE

AVERAGE INCOME

MAY STRUGGLE TO SEE RELEVANCE

LOWER

MAY NOT OWN HIS OWN BIBLE

WHAT KIDS THINK ABOUT THE BIBLE

HIGHER

CAN SEE A LACK OF NEED DUE TO ABUNDANCE OF RESOURCES

WHAT KIDS THINK ABOUT GOD

AVERAGE INCOME

SEES A NEED BUT UNSURE IF GOD IS TRUE

LOWER

MAY STRUGGLE TO TRUST GOD IN ALL SITUATIONS

63

LOWER

MAY NEED YOU TO NOTICE HER

AVERAGE INCOME

USUALLY HAVE ADEQUATE ATTENTION

HIGHER

MAY TEND TO DOMINATE SITUATIONS IN ORDER TO GET NOTICED

WHAT KIDS THINK ABOUT ATTENTION

Attention: Kids who need attention are obvious. Focus on giving positive attention to every child regardless of income.

Love: Define love as an emotion. Don't make blanket statements like "Your mom loves you" for kids whose experience hasn't shown this statement to be true.

Confidence: Plan sessions that have a variety of skills needed so that every kid can succeed.

MINISTRY IMPLICATIONS

Emotions

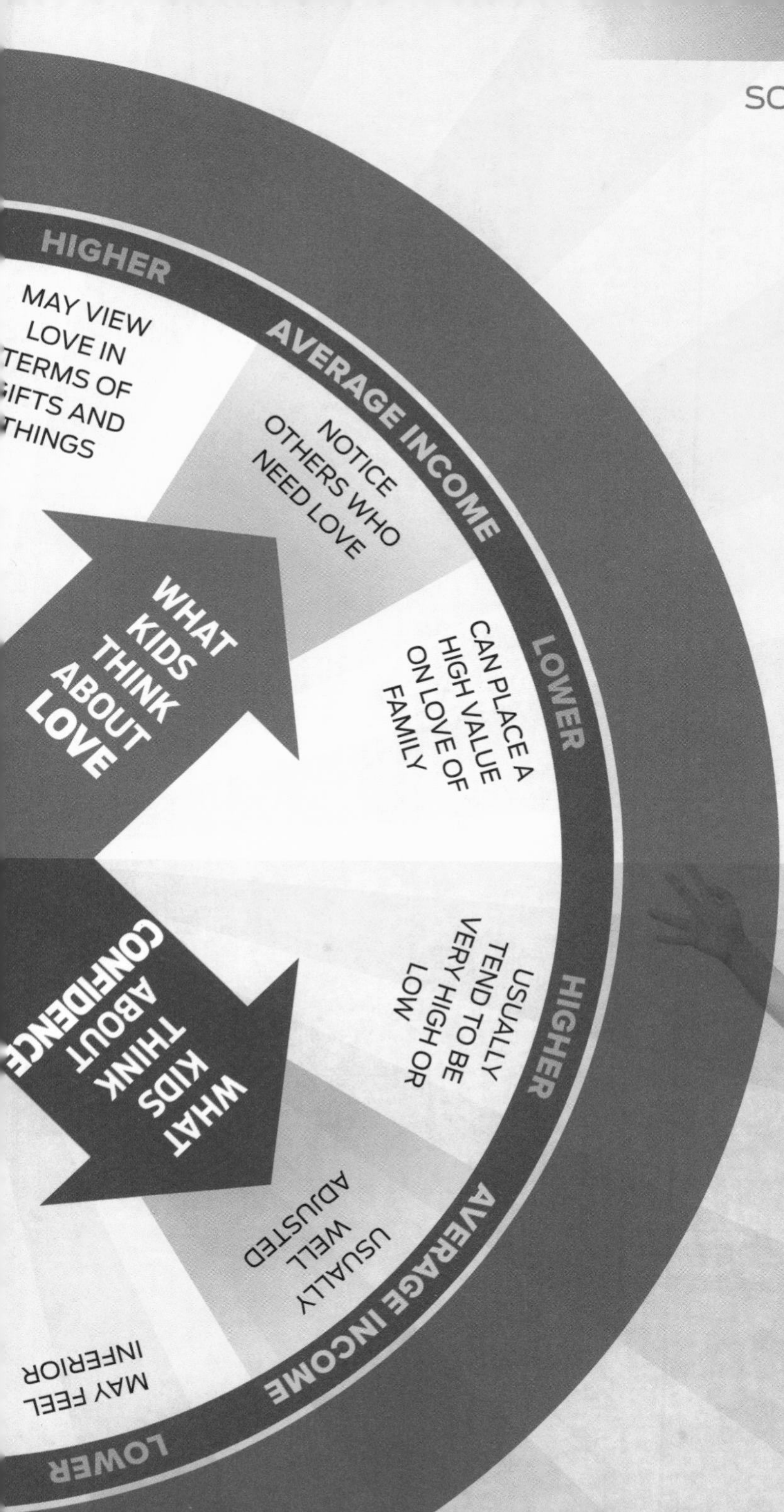

HIGHER

MAY VIEW LOVE IN TERMS OF GIFTS AND THINGS

AVERAGE INCOME

NOTICE OTHERS WHO NEED LOVE

LOWER

WHAT KIDS THINK ABOUT LOVE

CAN PLACE A HIGH VALUE ON LOVE OF FAMILY

HIGHER

USUALLY TEND TO BE VERY HIGH OR LOW

WHAT KIDS THINK ABOUT CONFIDENCE

AVERAGE INCOME

USUALLY WELL ADJUSTED

LOWER

MAY FEEL INFERIOR

Increasingly, kids are bringing their handheld video games to church. This doesn't mean that kids should play their video games while you teach. Plan your sessions to make them interactive and age appropriate. Do creative things to keep every kid's attention.

TELEVISION

Don't be surprised when kids tell you what they watch on TV. Avoid making judgment calls by saying "I would never allow my child to watch that," but help kids see how to make good choices in television.

All Kids

CLOTHES

Don't get caught up in what kids are wearing. Sometimes you can inadvertently alienate kids by focusing on neatly dressed kids.

ETHNICITY

While it might seem apparent, be careful to not make statements about other ethnicities. As churches become more diverse, be careful to welcome all of God's children.

YOU

Remember that you will bring all of your own biases into the classroom. Ask God to help you see each kid as a unique part of His creation.

APPROACHES TO
LEARNING

Everyone has a way he learns best. Kids are no different. Your 3-year-old has a few ways that help him learn better, just as your fourth grader also has ways that help her learn better. Generally, you might have one or two approaches that you tend to find are more dominant or preferred ways of learning. Because each person is unique, each one might have several different approaches which help him or her learn better.

TEACHING VISUAL LEARNERS ABOUT GOD

- Use lots of pictures and biblically accurate illustrations.
- Show maps.
- Build models of Bible-times structures.
- Allow kids to observe God's beauty in nature.
- Don't talk too much. Allow time for observation.

I love blocks and building.
I build forts and create
things from sticks and boxes.
I am a painter and sculptor.
I love to play with clay.
I love media and watching videos.
I can design posters, arrange
flowers, and think spatially.
I am a peoplewatcher
and can identify people easily.
I think in terms of pictures.

TEACHING NATURAL
LEARNERS ABOUT GOD

- Take frequent nature walks and encourage kids to engage in the study of natural things.
- Invite kids to plant something and allow them to take care of it.
- Collect nature items to help tell the story of God's creation.
- Use nature items to create pictures or illustrations of biblical events.

Natural

I enjoy the beauty of God's creation.

I easily learn to identify elements of the natural world.

I relate well to stories that allude to nature.

I love to investigate, explore, and study natural things.

I have a high sensitivity for taking care of the natural world.

TEACHING MUSICAL LEARNERS ABOUT GOD

- Encourage kids to make up songs about the Bible and its truths.
- Download Christian music and play it for your kids.
- Find music that helps enforce the truth you are teaching.
- Allow kids to play with musical instruments or make musical instruments from various items.
- Play music for kids while they are playing or working individually.

I AM A MOVER AND TOUCHER.

I KNOW THE WORLD THROUGH MY MUSCLES.

I ENJOY BUILDING MODELS, SWINGING, AND LEARNING SIGN LANGUAGE.

I AM A GREAT CHEERLEADER, AND I KNOW WHEN TO STICK OR SLIDE IN BASEBALL.

I HANDLE OBJECTS DEFTLY AND MAKE THINGS.

TEACHING PHYSICAL LEARNERS ABOUT GOD

- Play lots of active games.
- Use movements while telling Bible stories.
- Allow kids to perform dramas based on Bible stories.
- Encourage kids to stand while playing review games.
- Build models of biblical scenes from different types of materials.

I like word puzzles.

Numbers are alive for me, like characters in a book.

I relish mental math-estimating, measuring, and calculating.

I like to sort, categorize, compare, contrast, organize..

I see patterns and reason easily.

Logical

TEACHING LOGICAL LEARNERS ABOUT GOD

- Encourage kids to use math skills to determine biblical times and dates of events by adding and subtracting.
- Allow kids to read over the directions and follow them closely.
- Teach kids using biblical puzzles, riddles, and brain teasers.
- Encourage kids to follow Bible timelines to understand the stories.
- Apply Bible concepts to real-life situations through "what if" scenarios.

TEACHING REFLECTIVE LEARNERS ABOUT GOD

- Allow kids time to read the Bible quietly to themselves.
- Encourage kids to write out Bible facts.
- Provide family histories of biblical people.
- Allow kids time to think through their responses.
- Tell kids what the point of the lesson is.

Reflective

I HAPPILY WORK ALONE AND CONTRIBUTE CONFIDENTLY TO A GROUP.

I KEEP A DIARY.

I LIKE TO RECORD MY DREAMS & REMEMBER THINGS THAT ARE IMPORTANT TO ME.

I AM CURIOUS ABOUT MY FAMILY TREE AND POUR OVER FAMILY ALBUMS.

I AM DRAWN TO AUTOBIOGRAPHIES.

TEACHING VERBAL LEARNERS ABOUT GOD

- Let kids read directly from the Bible.
- Talk to kids about Bible times, facts, and stories.
- Play word games with kids.
- Allow kids to share their thoughts and opinions about Go
- Encourage kids to memorize Scripture passages.

I COLLECT NEW WORDS AND LOVE TO SHOW OFF MY VOCABULARY

I LIKE JOKES AND TONGUE TWISTERS

I LOVE AUDIOBOOKS

I make and keep a wide variety of friends.

I am the peacemaker on the playground.

No birthday party would be complete without me,
but I am not always the center of attention.

I'm a good listener, taking in everything from the sidelines.

I like to read biographies.

84

Relational

TEACHING RELATIONAL LEARNERS ABOUT GOD

- Allow kids to participate in group work.
- Give kids opportunities to socialize.
- Encourage kids to discuss Bible facts with each other.
- Provide time for kids to discuss problems.

CREATING
A LEARNING
ENVIRONMENT

The learning environment is the place where you teach. Every learning environment can be different, but here are some ideas for creating an environment where kids want to learn.

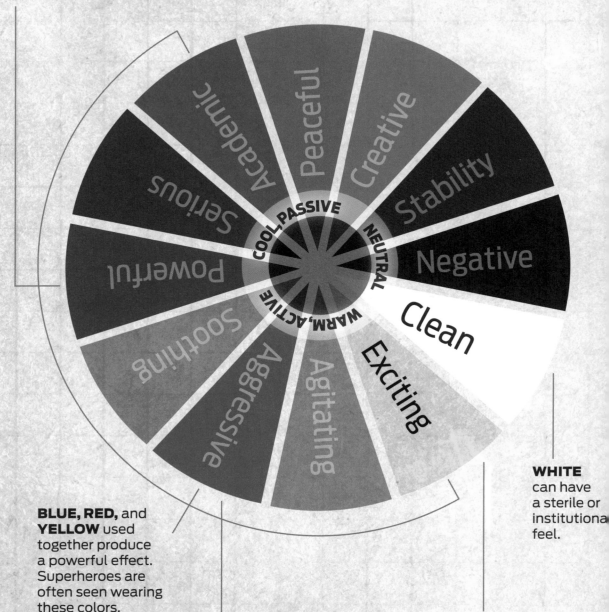

PURPLE is very appealing to children. It is one of the most preferred colors.

BLUE, RED, and **YELLOW** used together produce a powerful effect. Superheroes are often seen wearing these colors.

The color **RED** is often known for causing hunger. Think about the color of your favorite fast food restaurant.

WHITE can have a sterile or institutional feel.

BRIGHT YELLOW excites the brain. Can you think of any fictional characters who are bright yellow?

Color wheel labels: Academic, Peaceful, Creative, Stability, Serious, Negative, Powerful, Clean, Soothing, Exciting, Aggressive, Agitating, COOL, PASSIVE, NEUTRAL, WARM, ACTIVE

Color

BABY ROOMS

Avoid colors that are traditionally associated with specific genders. Opt for a soft peach, yellow, or green. Consider using a neutral color for three walls with a soft, bright accent wall.

TODDLER ROOMS

Use softer colors as opposed to bold coloring.

PRESCHOOL ROOMS

Begin to use deeper tones of the soft colors used with babies and toddlers.

YOUNGER KIDS ROOMS

Create an accent focal wall by using a bold, jewel-tone wall with three neutral-colored walls.

OLDER KIDS ROOMS

Neutral walls with bold splashes of color will create a modern exciting feel.

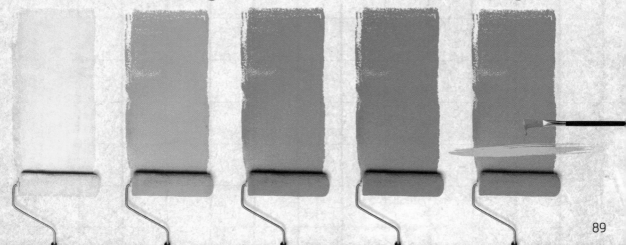

THIS IS YOUR FIRST CHANCE TO MAKE AN IMPACT. Invest time in making sure that your hallways and welcome center truly welcome kids and parents to the area. Parents love to see that their children will be learning in an exciting environment. Use appropriate colors from the list on pages 88-89.

Paintings and murals look great ... for a little while. Avoid permanent artwork when possible. It looks good for a time, but eventually everyone tires of it. Think about the permanence of paint. If the artist is a church member, it can really hurt her feelings when you paint over her masterpiece. Instead, if you would like to use murals, paint them on large wall hangings that can be interchanged.

Hallways and Welcome Center

Install **TELEVISIONS** to share announcements, usic, and add color to the hallways.

Hang **COLORFUL BANNERS** in the hallways or colorful fabrics in a flowing fashion along the ceiling.

Name the ministry and create a **LOGO** for it.

Use large **ACRYLIC POSTER** holders to hang photographs and other posters.

Create a moving feel with a **BOLD STRIPE** of color on the walls.

Use eye-catching **CARPETING** with a fun design.

Primary colors tend to lose appeal after a short period of time. Use **JEWEL TONES**.

THE IDEAL CLASSROOM

IDEALLY, ROOMS WOULD BE LARGE, RECTANGULAR SPACES with high ceilings, but the reality is that many rooms are narrow rectangles, L-shaped, and perhaps even wall-less. Working in an oddly-shaped or too-small room isn't impossible. Consider these options to use space creatively:

TOO SMALL
Create square-footage. Take furniture out until you feel like there is enough space for you and the kids. Furniture takes up lots of valuable space and you might not have it to spare.

TOO BIG
Reduce square-footage by concentrating all teaching and activities to a limited area.

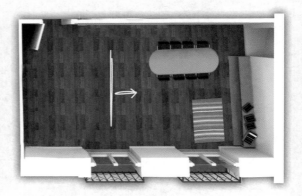

MULTIPLE AGE GROUPS IN THE SAME SPACE
Create classes using tents or room dividers. Divide the room into quadrants. Assign each age group a specific quadrant.

SHARING SPACE?
Avoid monopolizing the walls with lots of posters and décor. Reduce the look of cluttered walls. Consider hanging a bed sheet over another teacher's posters to create your own focal wall effect.

MEETING IN A NONTRADITIONAL OR BORROWED SPACE
Create a more secure-feeling environment by taping off room boundaries.

Classroom Space

UNIQUELY SHAPED

For oddly-shaped classrooms, focus on the largest portion of the area. Consider moving unnecessary items to the smallest part of the area to block it off and visually define where teaching will occur.

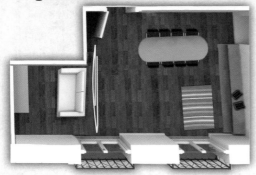

THE DREAM VS. THE REALITY

Check out the recommended space for different age groups and list the reality of space for your church:

AGE GROUP	SPACE PER PERSON		MAXIMUM ATTENDANCE		ROOM SIZE	
	DREAM	REALITY	DREAM	REALITY	DREAM	REALITY
BABIES	35 sq.ft.		12		420 sq.ft.	
ONES-TWOS	35 sq.ft.		12		420 sq.ft.	
PRE-SCHOOL	35 sq.ft.		16		560 sq.ft.	
YOUNGER KIDS	25 sq.ft.		20		600 sq.ft.	
OLDER KIDS	20 sq.ft.		24		480 sq.ft.	

CHAIRS

Buy chairs of the same color for different age groups so you alwa[y]s know which chairs belong in particular classrooms.

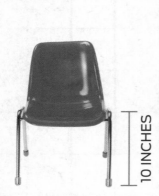

10 INCHES

ONES–TWOS

12 INCHES

PRESCHOOL

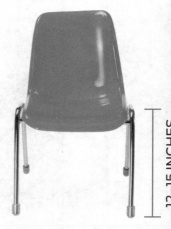

12–15 INCHES

YOUNGER KIDS

TEMPERATURE

Rooms should be neither too hot, nor too cold. An appropriate temperature for learning is 70-75 degrees.

TABLES

Tabletops for kids should be 10 inches above the chair seats.

10 INCHES

Classroom Environment

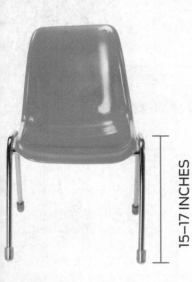

15–17 INCHES

OLDER KIDS

NOISE

Different activities call for different noise levels. Establish a quiet area for kids who do not function well in loud environments.

LIGHTING

Use an appropriate level of lighting. Kids function best in brightly lit rooms.

RULES

Avoid having a large list of rules. Instead focus on 3 to 4 key behavioral requests that all kids know and understand are to be followed in the classroom.

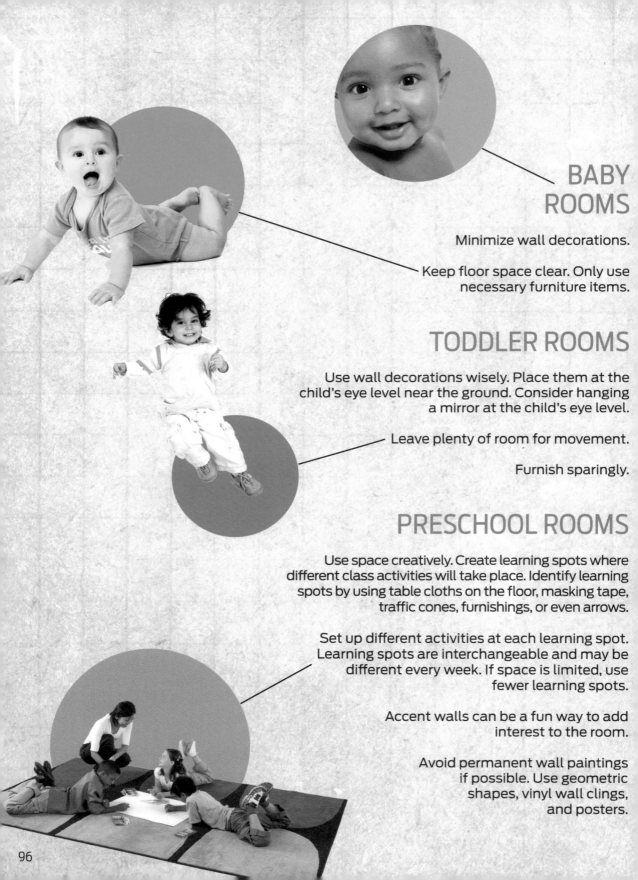

BABY ROOMS

Minimize wall decorations.

Keep floor space clear. Only use necessary furniture items.

TODDLER ROOMS

Use wall decorations wisely. Place them at the child's eye level near the ground. Consider hanging a mirror at the child's eye level.

Leave plenty of room for movement.

Furnish sparingly.

PRESCHOOL ROOMS

Use space creatively. Create learning spots where different class activities will take place. Identify learning spots by using table cloths on the floor, masking tape, traffic cones, furnishings, or even arrows.

Set up different activities at each learning spot. Learning spots are interchangeable and may be different every week. If space is limited, use fewer learning spots.

Accent walls can be a fun way to add interest to the room.

Avoid permanent wall paintings if possible. Use geometric shapes, vinyl wall clings, and posters.

Room Décor

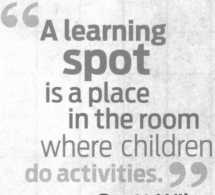

> **A learning spot** is a place in the room where children do activities.
> — Scott Wiley

YOUNGER KIDS

Magnetic and chalkboard paint can add interesting effects to the walls for a fun touch.

Avoid positioning your focal wall in the direction of the door. This is distracting to the kids.

If a more permanent visual pop is desired, consider painting silhouettes of complementary colors or geometric shapes.

Leave a large open space for active games and activities.

OLDER KIDS

Use furnishings with a comfortable and modern feel.

Magnetic and chalkboard paint can add interesting effects to the walls for a fun touch.

Use video media and computers to enhance the learning experience.

Leave a large open space for active games and activities.

THE TEACHER IS ULTIMATELY RESPONSIBLE for creating the learning environment. No matter where you meet—a classroom, a movie theater, or under a tree—the things you do to foster learning create the biggest impact. As a teacher, you should be:

Growing in your walk with Christ and theologically sound.

Committed to reaching kids in your class and enthusiastic about teaching them.

Interested in the things that interest kids.

Willing to build relationships with kids and their parents.

Prepared to teach through a time of prayer and planning.

The Teacher in the Learning Environment

Excited to teach kids using a variety learning approaches.

Understanding of the variety of socioeconomic backgrounds kids come from.

Accepting of all kids.

Teaching from an overflow of what God has taught you.

Able to learn, grow, and try new things; flexible and a team player.

7-DAY TEACHER PREP PLAN

This Week

Sunday READ THE SCRIPTURE PASSAGE FOR NEXT WEEK FROM YOUR BIBLE.

Monday READ THE SESSION POINT AND ANY BIBLICAL BACKGROUND INFORMATION.

Tuesday READ THE TEACHING PROCEDURES AND BEGIN GATHERING SUPPLIES.

Wednesday PRAY FOR SUNDAY SCHOOL KIDS AND CONTACT ANY KIDS WHO MISSED LAST SUNDAY.

Thursday REREAD THE SCRIPTURE PASSAGE. COMPLETE GATHERING SUPPLIES.

Friday PRAY FOR YOUR TEACHING TEAM AND CONNECT WITH THEM ABOUT WHO WILL DO WHAT.

Saturday REVIEW THE SCRIPTURE PASSAGE AND TEACHING PROCEDURES.

2-DAY TEACHER PREP PLAN

DAY 1
* READ THE SCRIPTURE PASSAGE AND BACKGROUND INFORMATION.
* READ THE TEACHING PROCEDURES.
* PRAY FOR KIDS.

DAY 2
* GATHER SUPPLIES.
* REREAD THE BIBLE STORY AND TEACHING PROCEDURES.

Teacher Preparation

1-HOUR TEACHER PREP PLAN

0 TO 15 MINUTES:
READ THE SCRIPTURE PASSAGE AND BIBLE STORY.

15 TO 45 MINUTES:
READ THE TEACHING PROCEDURES AND GATHER SUPPLIES.

45 TO 60 MINUTES:
PRAY AND REREAD BIBLE STORY.

> "The **best** session is a **planned** session."
>
> —Bill Emeott

TIPS FOR PLANNING:

1. Always make Scripture your starting point.
2. Don't feel like you have to do every activity.
3. Know your group. Some activities just won't work with them.
4. If you are in a time crunch, scan the prep list for items you already have.
5. Keep kids moving. Plan an active session!

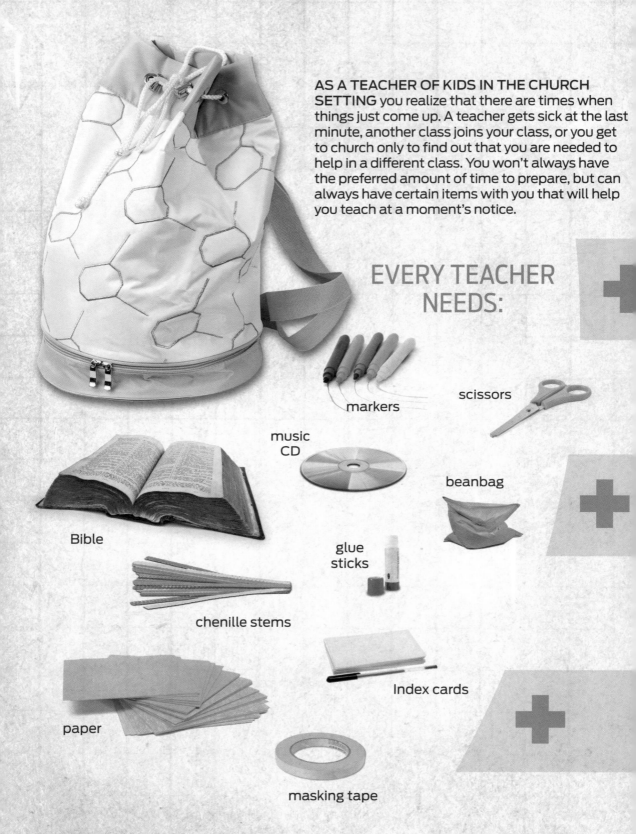

AS A TEACHER OF KIDS IN THE CHURCH SETTING you realize that there are times when things just come up. A teacher gets sick at the last minute, another class joins your class, or you get to church only to find out that you are needed to help in a different class. You won't always have the preferred amount of time to prepare, but can always have certain items with you that will help you teach at a moment's notice.

EVERY TEACHER NEEDS:

markers

scissors

music CD

beanbag

Bible

glue sticks

chenille stems

Index cards

paper

masking tape

The Prepared Leader

BABIES–TWOS TEACHERS ALSO NEED:

crayons

rattles

hand-size soft balls

large stickers

age-appropriate hand-size cars

picture books

PRESCHOOL TEACHERS ALSO NEED:

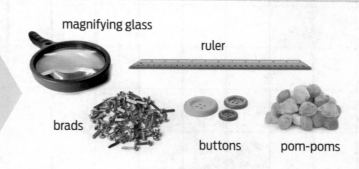

magnifying glass

ruler

brads

buttons

pom-poms

KIDS TEACHERS ALSO NEED:

ruler

ball

play dough

craft book

brads

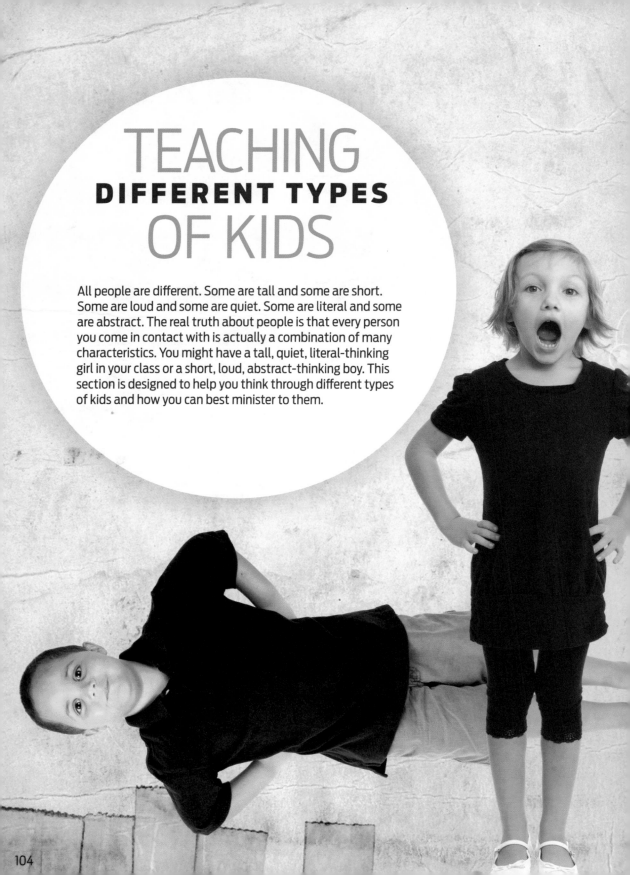

TEACHING
DIFFERENT TYPES
OF KIDS

All people are different. Some are tall and some are short. Some are loud and some are quiet. Some are literal and some are abstract. The real truth about people is that every person you come in contact with is actually a combination of many characteristics. You might have a tall, quiet, literal-thinking girl in your class or a short, loud, abstract-thinking boy. This section is designed to help you think through different types of kids and how you can best minister to them.

THERE IS NO WAY TO ADEQUATELY COVER exactly how to minister to each kid with learning differences or disabilities. As you have seen throughout this book, every kid is different and created in the image of God. Kids with special needs each have their own unique set of special characteristics.

1.

Get to know him. Don't be afraid you might say or do the wrong thing. Talk to him, ask him about his interests, and be patient with him. Every kid needs to be loved and accepted.

2.

Ask her parents what they would like for you to know about their child. Some kids with special needs have dietary or physical limitations. Remember these limitations as you plan your sessions.

3.

Be willing to learn about his unique needs. Explore ways you can remove any barriers due to a special medical condition. Talk to the parents and learn about what makes him so special.

Ministering to Kids with Special Needs

"Successfully including a child with special needs may require patience and repetition. I like to say, 'First time failure. Second time success,' meaning that you shouldn't be surprised when a child with unique needs struggles during his first visit. But just because the first experience was rough, it doesn't mean he can't be successful in that setting. Kids with learning differences or cognitive disabilities often acclimate after trial and error, as well as familiarity. Expect for it to take a little time to figure out what strategies work best for a particular child, and then give them the freedom to grow comfortable in a new setting."
—Amy Fenton Lee, "The Inclusive Church"

4.
Include her. When planning a special event or outing, be willing to go out of your way to make sure she is included and has a great time. This will take more time, but it will speak volumes to her and her parents.

5.
Pray for him. Ask God to allow you to be his champion. Ask Him to shine through you to this child and his parents.

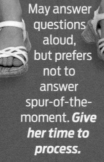
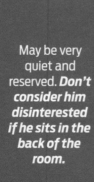

INTROVERT

May be very quiet and reserved. **Don't consider him disinterested if he sits in the back of the room.**

May answer questions aloud, but prefers not to answer spur-of-the-moment. **Give her time to process.**

Call him by name when asking a question. **He wants to answer, but not if he isn't called upon.**

May have times and situations in which she is more or less introverted or extroverted. **Consider how your class is organized to determine if a different approach might be beneficial.**

Introverts & Extroverts

Will freely express her thoughts with others. *Allow time for group discussion.*

Tends to speak while he thinks. *Guide the conversation back to the topic as it might easily go in a different direction.*

Energized in large groups. *She may be disengaged during individual assignments but thrive during group work.*

EXTROVERT

FOLLOWER

May seem outgoing, but she tends to shut down when asked to lead a group or work independently. *Develop confidence by complimenting her ability to lead or produce good work.*

May be drawn to a controlling kid as a friend. *Watch to make sure that he isn't taken advantage of by the bossy friend.*

May have an opinion about an activity, but seems to go with the crowd. *Watch for times when you think he might want to do something different than his peers.*

Followers & Leaders

May be more likely to be a leader if it is something she is good at, or a follower if she isn't familiar with it. *Use activities that require a different skill set.*

Develop a special code or symbol with him to help him recognize when he is being too vocal. Younger kids go through this phase as they learn how to give orders. *Limit the amount of attention you give to this bossy behavior.*

Can take over conversations. *Call on other kids to give input.*

May dominate activities. *Limit the amount of competition in group projects and games.*

LEADER

May dominate review games and activities. *Ask him to allow others the chance to answer.*

May only share the "Sunday School" answers to every question. *Encourage her to practically apply biblical truths.*

Has a good knowledge of church behavior guidelines but may not have a great knowledge of spiritual things. *Don't embarrass a child by saying things like "You should know this, you are here all the time!"*

May attend sporadically due to single-parent visitation, sports, schedules, and failute to prioritize. *Realize every time a child comes to your class is an opportunity for you to share Christ's love with her.*

Regulars & Uninformed

May appear to be shy and cautious about participating. *Partner her with a regular to make her feel more comfortable.*

May attempt to answer questions with off-the-wall answers. *Do not allow others to laugh if the answer seems silly. Help guide the child to discover the correct answer.*

Can be a behavior problem if unfamiliar with rules and expectations. *Take a few moments to share classroom expectations with the entire group.*

UNINFORMED

CLASS CLOWN

Will deliberately misbehave in order to get a laugh out of fellow classmates. *Avoid providing negative or positive attention to this behavior.*

May tend to make fun of himself. *Affirm him and his good work.*

May say things just to make people laugh. *Help her to know when this type of response is appropriate.*

Class Clowns & Pleasers

May be a healthy mixture of both characteristics. Kids who don't take themselves too seriously can be refreshing. *Don't neglect giving her some attention.*

Likes to be called upon. She tries to give the response she thinks you want. *Help her to know that it is OK to develop her own ideas by asking her to personalize her response to something she would do or say.*

May get upset when you do not recognize his good work. *Don't forget to recognize the kids who always have appropriate behavior.*

May seem unbelievably compliant. Arrives early and stays late. Volunteers to do everything. *Thank him for his help, but encourage him to loosen up and hang out with his peers.*

PLEASERS

BULLY

Not afraid to hit or pick-on another kid in your presence. *Remove the bully from the situation and discuss his actions with his parents if necessary.*

May display aggressive behavior toward the other kids in the class. *Help her know how to apologize to kids she may wrong.*

Can speak harshly to you or other kids in the class. *Remind him that he must speak respectfully to everyone.*

Can easily be both the bullied and the bully. *Help kids avoid bullying behavior in your class by setting an example of mutual respect.*

Bullies & Bullied

May be anxious around one or two kids who have singled her out as their target. *Give her techniques for diffusing the bullying situation on her own.*

May enjoy church, but does not attend special events or gatherings with less structured agendas. *Develop a way for him to quietly signal you if he feels threatened.*

Tends to have noticeable physical, social, mental, or emotional differences from others in class. *Watch out for her, coach her, and help her, but avoid becoming her constant rescuer.*

BULLIED

PERFECTIONIST

May become emotional when he makes mistakes or isn't the best. **Don't be critical. He is good enough at finding his own faults.**

May avoid doing tasks that she thinks she can't do to the exact specifications. **Point out times in your own life or teaching that you have made a mistake.**

May start tasks over when he makes an error. **Challenge him to fix his mistake without starting over.**

Perfectionists & Disinterested

May seem to show great interest at times and little to no interest at other times. *Vary your teaching methods so that in a single session you will do some things that each kid enjoys.*

May be more afraid of what his friends say than showing genuine disinterest. *Draw him into activities by creating new groups or allowing him to be a team captain.*

May seem to be somewhere else. Not necessarily daydreaming, but consumed with other thoughts. *Talk with her and learn about what is bothering her.*

May complain that activities are boring or behave inappropriately to cause distractions. *Ask him what you can do to make the class more interesting. Incorporate his ideas.*

DISINTERESTED

INSECURE

Needs constant approval and accolades. Can appear to be the teacher's pet. *Be careful to show attention to every child and encourage him to keep trying.*

May be very quiet and nonparticipatory. *Foster new friendships by pairing up kids to work together on certain projects.*

Slowly adjusts to new teachers and environments. *Avoid moving to different class locations. Keep furnishings in familiar places.*

May be more confident when regularly attending the same classroom with the same teacher. *Keep things as consistent as possible.*

Insecure & Confident

Willingly enters the room without clinging to parents. *Welcome her to class and have an activity ready for her to begin.*

Makes eye contact and speaks clearly. *Foster this confidence by giving him extra class responsibilities.*

Walks in with great posture, friendly, and outgoing. *Remember to notice her. Because of her good attitude and willingness, she can sometimes be overlooked.*

CONFIDENT

DISTRACTED

Can't seem to concentrate on anything. May act hyper in class. *Be patient with her. Plan lots of short activities to keep her moving.*

Asks random questions in the middle of the Bible story that have nothing to do with the story. *Explain that you will be happy to answer his question at the end of the story.*

May walk away from a task or activity before it is complete. *Ask her why she didn't want to finish. Offer to help her finish the activity.*

Completes tasks in a timely manner, but might get bored with overly simple activities. *Keep things moving.*

Distracted & Focused

Vary the skill level of activities for each session. **Make sure to provide challenging activities for every kid.**

Seems to hang onto your words and may get annoyed when someone is distracting. **Thank her for listening well, and remind her to be patient with the other kids.**

Will not move on from the task or activity until it is complete. **Give warnings several minutes prior to the end of the activity so he can know he needs to wrap up his work.**

FOCUSED

SNAPSHOTS
INDEX OF
WHOLLY KIDS

Physical Characteristics TIMELINE

4 FOURS
show good large muscle coordination
develop a longer, leaner body
develop fine motor control
exhibit right- and left-handedness

B BABIES
use many complex reflexes
begin to reach toward objects
hold up their heads
sit, roll over, crawl

3 THREES
use large muscles
dress themseves fairly easily
display some fine motor skills
dislike nap time and have difficulty sleeping during this time

1 ONES
climb
love to explore
draw on paper with markers
carry objects from place to place

2 TWOS
develop preference for right or left hand
stand on one foot and balance
have better gross motor coordination
help undress themselves

Babies   Ones   Twos   Threes   Fours   Fives   Sixes

FIVES

skip well; hop in a straight line
display good hand-eye coordination
exhibit well-established right- or left-handedness
can control their large muscles
develop appetites for favorite foods

SIXES

ppy, in a hurry; speed is a benchmark
arning to distinguish left from right
tire easily
suffer frequent illness
enjoys outdoors, gym

NINES

have slow, steady growth
good muscle control
girls' bodies usually develop more
quickly than boys

TENS

like to use abundant energy
and physical skills

ELEVENS

have good coordination and muscle skills

SEVENS

sometimes tense
like confined space
many hurts, real and imagined

EIGHTS

have good hand-eye
coordination
may overdo it with physical
activities and have trouble
calming down

TWELVES

are approaching puberty; girls
usually develop ahead of boys

Sevens   Eights   Nines   Tens   Elevens   Twelves

FIVES

can print name, but not too clearly
utilize a 2,000-word vocabulary
seek explanations concerning why and how
begin to recognize basic reading words
enjoy classification, sequencing, and sorting

FOURS

have increased attention span
are highly imaginative; cannot separate fact and fantasy
use 500 to 2,000 words
enjoy being silly
use many words without knowing their meanings

THREES

use 300 to 1,000 words
display creativity and imagination
begin speaking in complete sentences
can only do one thing at a time

TWOS

use 5 to 300 words
begin using sentences
identify themselves by gender
follow simple directions in order
begin using numbers
know colors

ONES

remember simple events
begin to group familiar objects
understand and use words for items
try to make themselves understood

BABIES

use senses to learn
recognize principle caregivers
use vocal and non-vocal communication
know and respond to name

SIXES
may like to work
may like to explain things; show-and-tell is useful
may love jokes and guessing games
love to ask questions
like new games, ideas
learn best through discovery

SEVENS
need closure, must complete assignments
may like to work slowly and alone
reflective ability growing
erase constantly, want work to be perfect
like to repeat tasks
want to discover how things work

EIGHTS
like to experiment and find out how things are made
vary with peers in reading ability
value money
are eager to learn

NINES
have lengthening attention span
accept carefully worded criticism
are beginning to think abstractly

TENS
are imaginative, creative, and curious
can express ideas, understand cause and effect,
solve problems, and plan

ELEVENS
are capable of deep thoughts
can cope with success and failure
can concentrate when interested
think quickly and memorize easily

TWELVES
can distinguish between fact and fiction
can accept and work toward short-term goals
can discern time and space relationships

Mental Characteristics
TIMELINE

Spiritual Characteristics
TIMELINE

BABIES

develop a sense of trust as needs are met consistently

sense attitudes and expressions of love

may point to the Bible and pictures of Jesus

THREES

can identify some Bible characters and stories

understand that God, Jesus, and church are special

begin to develop a conscience and are sensitive to feelings of shame and guilt

SIXES

see Jesus as a friend and helper

like learning from the Bible and know many basic Bible stori

may make conclusions about God

may begin to have a simple understanding of sin

may begin to have a simple understanding of the gospel

know the right answers but may not understand applicatio

EIGHTS

ask serious questions about religion

are developing values

can be truthful and honest

often have difficulty making decisions

NINES

are often beginning to feel the need for a Savior

are growing conscious of themselves and of sin

want to do things the right way and think in terms of right and wrong more than good and evil

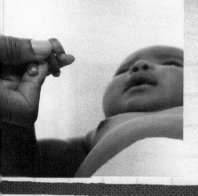

ONES

grow in trust of adults

begin to distinguish between acceptable and unacceptable behavior

begin to recognize simple pictures of Jesus

TWOS

can sing simple songs about God and Jesus

can say thank You to God

can listen to Bible stories

FOURS

like to retell Bible stories

recognize that God and Jesus love people and help people in special ways

exhibit a conscience

express love for God and Jesus

FIVES

remember and like to tell Bible stories

use the Bible and like to find Bible phrases/verses

begin to ask questions about God

can make life application of Bible verses

SEVENS

may be interested in finding out more about God and Jesus

may ask why God would let Jesus die for the wrong things that everyone else does

may recognize consequences for their sin

may understand that people become Christians by accepting Jesus as Savior and Lord

TENS

are developing concepts of love and trust

are developing a conscience and a value system

ELEVENS

have formed concepts of personal worth

are ready for spiritual answers and directions

can make many choices, but may not follow through on long-term commitments

TWELVES

feel deeply about own experiences

beginning to adopt a religious belief system of their own

9

NINES
need to be able to let off
steam and may take out
feelings on others
are beginning to feel that the
group is as important as self
are great talkers and need to
be allowed to talk

10

are motivated most by own
interest and think of themselv
can operate comfortably with
a group
like acceptance and
encouragement; can become
easily discouraged

ELEVENS
can accept rules, organizatior

TENS

8

EIGHTS
like peers of the same sex
and dislike the opposite sex
like to work with others

Social/
Emotional
Characteristics
TIMELINE

7

SEVENS
sometimes moody, depressed,
sulking, or shy
need security, structure
sensitive to others' feelings
can be conscientious and serious
have strong likes and dislikes

6

5

SIXES
are competitive; enthusiastic
are sometimes a poor sport or dishonest; invent rules
view any failure as hard, thrive on encouragement
are easily upset when hurt
friends are important (may have a best friend)

FIVES
get along well in small groups
have best friends, but change friends often
may be prone to self-criticism and guilt
begin to distinguish truth from lies
can accept responsibility

11 responsibilities, and leader-
follower roles
like to win and improve on
achievements
recognize and appreciate
individual differences

TWELVES
are aware of sex roles; have

12 changing attitudes toward the opposite
sex
have deep need for companionship and
approval of peers
are easily influenced emotionally and
can cope with some feelings

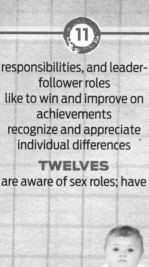

B

BABIES
show alertness when talked to
begin to initiate social interchange
become quiet in unfamiliar settings
make eye contact and smile at others
show interest in other children

ONES
experience stranger anxiety
play simple games
can practice taking turns
recognize others' emotions

1

TWOS
take interest in family
initiate play with peers
can be loving and affectionate
strongly assert independence

2

4

3

FOURS
have total confidence in their own abilities
tattle frequently
focus on cooperative play and take turns
like to be helpers if they initiate the idea
respond to reason, humor, and firmness

THREES
try to please adults; conform more often
respond to verbal guidance
enjoy encouragement
play cooperatively with others

Girls are more able to focus when they are sitting in a warmer room. **FOCUS**

Girls may shy away from risk. **RISK**

Girls are drawn more toward colors. **VISUAL APPEAL**

Girls learn best through words. **LEARNING**

Girls enjoy reading and writing. **READING**

Girls develop fine motor skills early. **MOTOR SKILLS**

Girls can thrive in larger groups. **GROUPS**

Girls find fiction books interesting. **BOOKS**

Girls can stay focused for longer periods each day. **FOCUS**

Girls have a less-developed spatial memory. **SPATIAL**

Girls grow more steadily and consistently. **GROWTH**

Girls show emotion and care about people's feelings. **FEELINGS**

Girls vs. Boys
COMPARISON CHART

FOCUS — Boys are able to focus more when they are standing in a cooler room.

RISK — Boys tend to be more daring.

VISUAL APPEAL — Boys are drawn toward moving objects.

LEARNING — Boys often learn better through pictures.

READING — Boys avoid reading and writing.

MOTOR SKILLS — Boys develop fine motor skills later.

GROUPS — Boys learn best in smaller groups.

BOOKS — Boys prefer books that are about real things or events.

FOCUS — Boys will zone out several times each day.

SPATIAL — Boys can more easily remember where things are placed.

GROWTH — Boys grow in spurts and are behind girls throughout most of childhood.

FEELINGS — Boys care less about feelings and people.

Socioeconomic Factors
CHART

HIGHER

RULES	May seem to disregard rules
HEROES	Tend to choose wealthy role models
EDUCATION	Can take opportunities for granted
CLOTHES	Almost always comes to church in something new
CHRISTMAS	May brag about receiving lots of loot
SPECIAL EVENTS	May place higher value on events that cost something
DIVORCED/SINGLE PARENT FAMILY	May not understand parents reason for divorce
BLENDED FAMILY	May play parents against each other
TRADITIONAL FAMILY	May seem like family has it all together
CHURCH	May expect more from her experience
GOD	Can see a lack of need due to abundance of resources
BIBLE	May bring Bible to class on electronic device
LOVE	May view love in terms of gifts and things
CONFIDENCE	Usually tends to be very high or low
ATTENTION	May tend to dominate situations in order to get noticed

AVERAGE INCOME	LOWER
Know why rules exist	Can see as a means of hindrance
Often choose famous heroes	May be more realistic in hero selection
Usually have supportive parental involvement	May need to be motivated
May compare his clothes to those who have more	May have one or two nice things he wears often
Parents may splurge at this time of year	Can be sensitive to the amount of toys received by peers
Struggle to keep up with too many options	May not have funds for events that cost
May know reason for parents divorce	May have never met father
Has definite opinions of stepsiblings	May have many people living in the same home
May have several siblings	May live with extended family members
May not place a priority on church	May feel like she doesn't fit in with your group
Sees a need but unsure if God is true	May struggle to trust God in all situations
May struggle to see relevance	May not own his own Bible
Notice others who need love	May place high value on love of family
Well adjusted	May feel inferior
Usually have adequate attention	May need you to notice her

Learning Approaches
What Kind
of **Learner**
Are You **?**

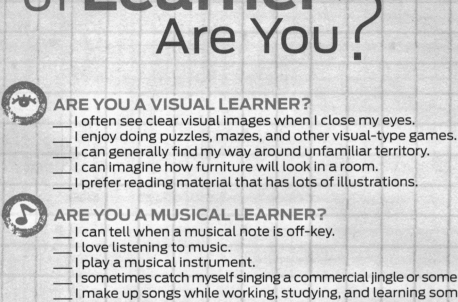

ARE YOU A VISUAL LEARNER?
___ I often see clear visual images when I close my eyes.
___ I enjoy doing puzzles, mazes, and other visual-type games.
___ I can generally find my way around unfamiliar territory.
___ I can imagine how furniture will look in a room.
___ I prefer reading material that has lots of illustrations.

ARE YOU A MUSICAL LEARNER?
___ I can tell when a musical note is off-key.
___ I love listening to music.
___ I play a musical instrument.
___ I sometimes catch myself singing a commercial jingle or some other tune
___ I make up songs while working, studying, and learning something ne

ARE YOU A LOGICAL LEARNER?
__ I can easily compute numbers in my head.
__ Math and/or science were among my favorite subjects in school.
__ I enjoy playing games or solving brain teasers that require logical thinkin
__ I like to set up "what if" experiments.
__ My mind searches for patterns, regularities, or logical sequences in thing
__ I like finding logical flaws in things people say and do at home and at work.
__ I feel more comfortable when something has been measured,
   categorized, or analyzed.

ARE YOU A VERBAL LEARNER?
__ Books are very important to me.
__ I can hear words in my head before I read, speak, or write them down.
__ I get more out of listening to the radio or a spoken-word audiobook
   than I do from television or videos.
__ I enjoy word games like Scrabble® or Password®.
__ English, social studies, and history are easier for me in school than
   math and science.
__ When I drive down a freeway, I pay more attention to the words writte
   on billboards than scenery.
__ My conversation includes frequent references to things I've read or hear

ARE YOU A PHYSICAL LEARNER?

__ I engage in a least one sport or physical activity on a regular basis.
__ I find it difficult to sit still for long periods of time.
__ I like working with my hands at concrete activities such as sewing, weaving, carving, or carpentry.
__ My best ideas often come to me when I'm out for a walk or jog or engaged in some other kind of physical activity.
__ I frequently use hand gestures or other forms of body language when conversing with someone.
__ I need to touch things in order to learn more about them.
__ I need to practice a new skill rather than simply reading about it or seeing a video.

ARE YOU A NATURAL LEARNER?

__ I like to spend time outdoors.
__ I enjoy collecting objects from nature.
__ I know the scientific names of many plants and animals.
__ My idea of relaxing is looking at a seed catalog or working in the yard.
__ My hobbies include taking care of plants and/or pets.

ARE YOU A RELATIONAL LEARNER?

__ I'm the sort of person that people come to for advice and counsel at work or in my neighborhood.
__ When I have a problem I'm more likely to seek out another person for help than attempt to work it out on my own.
__ I favor social pastimes such as group games over solitary recreation.
__ I enjoy the challenge of teaching another person, or groups of people, what I know how to do.
__ I like to get involved in social activities connected with my work, church, or community.
__ I would rather spend my evening at a lively party than stay at home alone.

ARE YOU A REFLECTIVE LEARNER?

__ I regularly spend time alone meditating, reflecting, or thinking about important life questions.
__ I have a special hobby or interest that I keep pretty much to myself.
__ I have a realistic view of my strengths and weaknesses.
__ I would prefer to spend a weekend alone in a cabin in the woods than at a fancy resort with lots of people around.
__ I consider myself to be strong-willed or independent-minded.
__ I keep a personal diary or journal to record the events of my life.

COLOR

Be creative and wisely use color in your classroom, hallways, and welcome center.

HALLWAYS

Consider spending the bulk of your time and budget on décor in the hallways and welcome center. This is the first point of contact for families.

CLASSROOM SPACE

Not all classrooms are created equal. Be creative and conscious of how to use your classroom space effectively.

CLASSROOM ENVIRONMENT

Proper chair and table height, suitable temperature, and attainable behavioral standards will all impact the level of success you have in creating an age-appropriate learning environment.

Creating a Learning Environment
SUMMARY

ROOM DÉCOR
Decorating your room is a great idea. Be mindful of how to share your space and consider how to make decorations more age-appropriate for the groups that use your class.

THE TEACHER
IN THE LEARNING ENVIRONMENT
The teacher is key to creating the learning environment.

TEACHER PREPARATION
Dedicate an appropriate amount of time to planning each week.

THE PREPARED LEADER
A leader can be successful in a spur-of-the-moment teaching opportunity when he has a few items ready ahead of time and adds a little creativity!

Adapting to Different Learners
SUMMARY

	HIGH	MEDIUM	LOW
INTROVERT	May be very quiet and reserved. Don't consider him disinterested if he sits in the back of the room..	May answer questions aloud, but prefers not to answer spur-of-the-moment. Give her time to process.	Call him by name when asking a question. He wants to answer, but not if he isn't called upon.
LEADER	May dominate activities. Limit the amount of competition in group projects and games.	Can take over conversations. Call on other kids to give input.	Develop a special code or symbol with him to help him recognize when he is being too vocal. Younger kids go through this phase as they learn how to give orders. Limit the amount of attention you give to this bossy behavior.
REGULARS	May dominate review games and activities. Ask him to allow others the chance to answer.	May only share the "Sunday School" answers to every question. Encourage her to practically apply biblical truths.	Has a good knowledge of church behavior guidelines but may not have a great knowledge of spiritual things. Don't embarrass a child by saying things like "You should know this, you are here all the time!"
CLASS CLOWN	Will deliberately misbehave in order to get a laugh out of fellow classmates. Avoid providing negative or positive attention to this behavior.	May tend to make fun of himself. Affirm him and his good work.	May say things just to make people laugh. Help her to know when this type of response is appropriate.
BULLY	Not afraid to hit or pick-on another kid in your presence. Remove the bully from the situation and discuss his actions with his parents if necessary.	May display aggressive behavior toward the other kids in the class. Help her know how to apologize to kids she may wrong.	Can speak harshly to you or other kids in the class. Remind him that he must speak respectfully to everyone.
CONFIDENT	Walks in with great posture, friendly, and outgoing. Remember to notice her. Because of her good attitude and willingness, she can sometimes be overlooked.	Makes eye contact and speaks clearly. Foster this confidence by giving him extra class responsibilities.	Willingly enters the room without clinging to parents. Welcome her to class and have an activity ready for her to begin.
PERFECTIONIST	May become emotional when he makes mistakes or isn't the best. Don't be critical. He is good enough at finding his own faults.	May avoid doing tasks that she thinks she can't do to the exact specifications. Point out times in your own life or teaching that you have made a mistake.	May start tasks over when he makes an error. Challenge him to fix his mistake without starting over.
DISTRACTED	Can't seem to concentrate on anything. May act hyper in class. Be patient with her. Plan lots of short activities to keep her moving.	Asks random questions in the middle of the Bible story that have nothing to do with the story. Explain that you will be happy to answer his question at the end of the story.	May walk away from a task or activity before it is complete. Ask her why she didn't want to finish. Offer to help her finish the activity.

AVERAGE	LOW	MEDIUM	HIGH	
May have times and situations in which he or she is more or less introverted or extroverted. Consider how your class is organized to determine if a different approach might be beneficial.	Will freely express her thoughts with others. Allow time for group discussion.	Tends to speak while he thinks. Guide the conversation back to the topic as it might easily go in a different direction.	Energized in large groups. She may be disengaged during individual assignments, but comes alive during group work.	EXTROVERT
May be more likely to be a leader if it is something she is good at, or a follower if she isn't familiar with it.	May have an opinion about an activity, but seems to go with the crowd. Watch for times when you think he might want to do something different than his immediate peers.	May be drawn to a controlling kid as a friend. Watch to make sure that he isn't taken advantage of by the bossy friend.	May seem outgoing, but tends to shut down when asked to lead a group or work independently. Develop confidence by complimenting her ability to lead or produce good work.	FOLLOWER
May attend sporadically due to single-parent visitation, sports, schedules, and failure to prioritize. Realize that every time a child comes to your class is an opportunity for you to share Christ's love with her.	May appear to be shy and cautious about participating. Partner her with a regular to make her feel more comfortable.	May attempt to answer questions with off-the-wall answers. Do not allow others to laugh if the answer seems silly. Help guide the child to discover the correct answer.	Can be a behavior problem if unfamiliar with rules and expectations. Take a few moments to share classroom expectations with the entire group.	UNINFORMED
May be a healthy mixture of both characteristics. Kids who don't take themselves too seriously can be refreshing.	Likes to be called upon. She tries to give the response she thinks you want. Help her to know that it is OK to develop her own ideas by asking her to personalize her response to something she would do or say.	May get upset when you do not recognize his good work. Don't forget to recognize the kids who always have appropriate behavior.	May seem unbelievably compliant. Arrives early and stays late. Volunteers to do everything. Thank her for her help, but encourage her to loosen up and hang out with her peers.	PLEASER
Can easily be both the bullied and the bully. Help kids avoid bullying behavior in your class by setting an example of mutual respect.	May be anxious around one or two kids who have singled her out as their target. Give her techniques for diffusing the bullying situation on her own.	May enjoy church, but does not attend special events or gatherings with less structured agendas. Develop a way for him to quietly signal you if he feels threatened.	Tends to have noticeable physical, social, mental, or emotional differences from others in class. Watch out for her, coach her, and help her, but avoid becoming her constant rescuer.	BULLIED
May be more confident when regularly attending the same classroom with the same teacher. Keep things as consistent as possible.	Slowly adjusts to new teachers and environments. Avoid moving to different class locations. Keep furnishings in familiar places.	May be very quiet and nonparticipatory. Foster new friendships by pairing up kids to work together on certain projects.	Needs constant approval and accolades. Can appear to be the teacher's pet. Be careful to show attention to every child.	INSECURE
May seem to show great interest at times and little to no interest at other times. Vary your teaching methods so that in a single session you will do some things that each kid enjoys.	May be more afraid of what his friends say than showing genuine disinterest. Draw him into activities by creating new groups or allowing him to be a team captain.	May seem to be somewhere else. Not necessarily daydreaming, but consumed with other thoughts. Talk with her and learn about what is bothering her. This may present a brand-new ministry opportunity.	May complain that activities are boring or behave inappropriately to cause distractions. Ask him what you can do to make the class more interesting. Incorporate his ideas.	DISINTERESTED
Completes tasks in a timely manner, but might get bored with overly simple activities.	Vary the skill level of activities for each session. Make sure to provide challenging activities for every kid.	Seems to hang onto your words and may get annoyed when someone is distracting. Thank her for listening well, and remind her to be patient with the other kids.	Will not move on from the task or activity until it is complete. Give warnings several minutes prior to the end of the activity so he can know he needs to wrap up his work.	FOCUSED

LifeWay | **Kids**

**Serving churches
in their mission
of making disciples**